To Dad & Fridebora Phillips
Love always,
Blessings From Terri & Mike

Happy New Year ~ 2014!
Wishing you love, happiness, peace & good health
in all ways! We love you both! We miss you, too!

The Song of the Sea

D. Morgan®

HARVEST HOUSE PUBLISHERS

EUGENE, OREGON

The Song of the Sea

Text Copyright © 1999 by Harvest House Publishers
Eugene, Oregon 97402
www.harvesthousepublishers.com

ISBN-13: 978-0-7369-2322-4

Artwork designs are reproduced under license from
© 2008 Leo Licensing, LLC and may not be
reproduced without permission. For more information
regarding art prints found in this book, please contact:

Leo Licensing
8573 Medlin Road
Baxter, TN 38544
931-838-1515
www.leolicensing.com

Design and production by Koechel Peterson & Associates, Minneapolis, Minnesota

Harvest House has made every effort to trace the ownership of all poems and quotes. In the event of a question arising from the use of a poem
or quote, we regret any error made and will be pleased to make the necessary correction in future editions of the book.

"The Singularity of Shells" by Luci Shaw, Copyright © Harold Shaw Publishers. Used by permission.

Scripture quotations are taken from The Living Bible, Copyright © 1971. Used by permission of Tyndale House Publishers, Inc., Wheaton, IL
60189 USA. All rights reserved; and from the New American Standard Bible. © 1960, 1962, 1963, 1968, 1971, 1972, 1975, 1977 by The
Lockman Foundation. Used by permission. (www.Lockman.org).

Printed in China

10 11 12 13 14 15 / IM / 10 9 8 7 6 5 4 3

I have made friends with the sea; it has taught me a great deal.
There is a kind of inspiration in the sea. When one listens to its never-ceasing murmur afar out there,
always sounding at midnight and mid-day, one's soul goes out to meet Eternity.

L.M. MONTGOMERY
Along the Shore

D. Morgan © 1990

All day to watch the

blue wave curl and break,

All night to hear it

plunging on the shore—

In this sea-dream

such draughts of life I take,

I cannot ask for more.

THOMAS BAILEY

This enduring romance ..... Our Love Affair With The Sea.

The voice of the sea speaks to the soul.

The touch of the sea is sensuous,

enfolding the body in its soft, close embrace.

KATE CHOPIN

D. Morgan © 1997

All I ask is a tall ship and a star to steer her by.

JOHN MASEFIELD

We are as near to heaven

by sea as by land!

SIR HUMPHREY GILBERT

I'd Rather...

D. Morgan

...Be Sailing.

D. Morgan © 1990

Gi'e me the ocean for my dower,

My vessel for my home.

Miss Corbett
"We'll Go to Sea No More"

Carolina . . . . .

To me there is something completely and satisfyingly restful

in that stretch of sea and sand, sea and sand and sky

complete peace and complete fulfillment.

ANNE MORROW LINDBERGH

*G*reat joy in camp we are in view of the Ocean...

this great Pacific Ocean which we have been so long anxious

to see. And the roaring or noise made by the waves breaking

on the rocky shores (as I suppose) may be heard distinctly.

WILLIAM CLARK
At Pillar Rock, Thursday, 7 November 1805

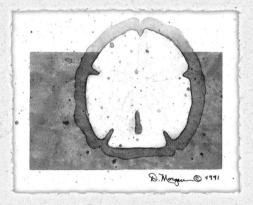

D. Morgan © 1991

......By

The

Sea.   D. Morgan © 1993

O mother, mother, hear the sea!

it calls across the sands;

I saw it tossing up the spray, like white,

imploring hands.

MARY ARTEMISIA LATHBURY

it's always ourselves we find in the sea.

e.e. cummings

D. Morgan ©1990

Hear the Sea

I feel your wet shifting sand ~

~ Taste your

And

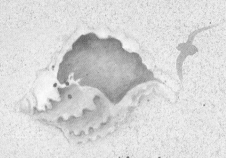

My soul is full of longing

For the secret of the sea,

And the heart of the great ocean

Sends a thrilling pulse through me.

HENRY WADSWORTH LONGFELLOW
"The Sound of the Sea"

sweet salty air ~

When anxious, uneasy and bad thoughts come,

I go to the sea, and the sea drowns them out with

its great wide sounds, cleanses me with its noise

and imposes a rhythm upon everything in me

that is bewildered and confused.

RAINER MARIA RILKE

I am renewed again .....

..... With the joy

Of

Living.

D. Morgan ©1993

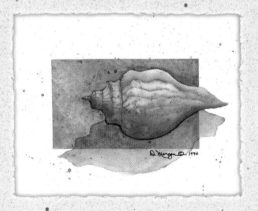

I must go down to the sea again,

for the call of the running tide

Is a wild call and a clear call

that may not be denied;

And all I ask is a windy day

with the white clouds flying,

And the flung spray and the blown spume,

and the sea-gulls crying.

JOHN MASEFIELD

*S*omewhere near the ocean,

Someplace by the sea—

On a silver ship or barnacle boat,

A fisherman's life for me.

D. MORGAN

"And what is the sea?" asked Will.

"The sea!" cried the miller.

"Lord help us all, it is the greatest thing God made!"

ROBERT LOUIS STEVENSON

D. Morgan ©1990

Pure

And ...

Serenity

... Simple.

D. Morgan © 1990

A life on the ocean wave!

A home on the rolling deep,

Where the scattered waters rave,

And the winds their revels keep!

EPES SARGENT

Many the wonders I this day have seen:

...The ocean with its vastness, its blue green,

Its ships, its rocks, its caves, its hopes, its fears, /

Its voice mysterious, which whoso hears

Must think on what will be, and what has been.

JOHN KEATS

No sooner had I been helped into

my bathing-suit than I sprang out upon

the warm sand and without thought

of fear plunged into the cool water.

I felt the great billows rock and sink.

The buoyant motion of the water

filled me with an exquisite, quivering joy.

HELEN KELLER

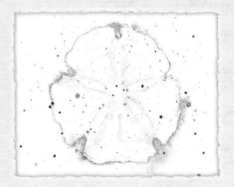

I could never stay long enough on the shore.

The tang of the untainted, fresh and free sea air

was like a cool, quieting thought,

and the shells and pebbles and the seaweed

with tiny living creatures attached to it

never lost their fascination for me.

HELEN KELLER

Heaven's a little closer

God, how great You are!

You stretched out the starry curtain of the heavens,

and hollowed out the surface of the earth to form the sea.

THE BOOK OF PSALMS

In a house.....

.... By the sea.

D. Morgan © 1990

Let the heavens be glad, the earth rejoice;

let the vastness of the roaring seas demonstrate his glory.

THE BOOK OF PSALMS

If I ride the morning winds to the farthest ocean,

even there your hand will guide me, your strength will support me.

THE BOOK OF PSALMS

God is with you... Always

1981 © D. Morgan

D. Morgan © 1990

I'm on the sea! I'm on the sea!

I am where I would ever be,

With the blue above and the blue below,

And silence wheresoe'er I go.

BRYAN W. PROCTOR

If my dreams could all come true
Paradise would be

~ In a little bungalow ~

Somewhere . . . .

I never was on the dull, tame shore,

But I loved the great sea more and more.

BRYAN W. PROCTOR

..... By the sea.   D. Morgan © 1993

From far away, a friendly light.

D. Morgan © 1994

I never see a gallant ship go steaming out to sea,

But what a little boy who was coming running back to me,

A little chap I thought was dead or lost forevermore,

Who used to watch the ships go out and long to quit the shore.

*H*e followed them to India, to China and Japan,

He told the flying sea gulls that he'd be a sailor-man.

"Some day," he said, "I'll own a ship and sail to Singapore,

And maybe bring a parrot back, or two or three or four."

*A*nd often when he went to bed, this little boy would lie

And fancy that the ceiling was a wide and starry sky;

The ocean was beneath him, and as happy as could be

He was master of a vessel that was putting out to sea.

EDGAR GUEST
"Sea Dreams"

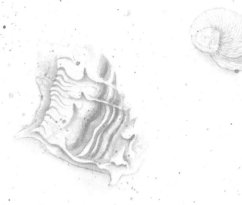

I Love thee, boundless Sea,

Thy ripples soft and mild,

So like the smiles that play

on lips of dreaming child.

FELIX O'NEILL

Lighthouse beacon in the night.

D. Morgan © 1994

D. Morgan © 1990

THE SEA SHELL

Sea shell, sea shell,

Sing me a song, oh, please

A song of ships and sailor-men

Of parrots and tropical trees;

Of islands lost in the Spanish Main

Which no man ever may see again,

Of fishes and corals under the waves,

And seashores stabled in great green caves—

Sea shell, sea shell,

Sing of the things you know so well.

AMY LOWELL

...that serene ocean rolled eastwards from me a thousand leagues of blue.

HERMAN MELVILLE, *Moby-Dick*

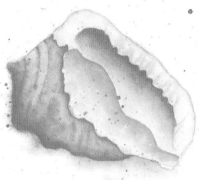

Those who go down to the sea in ships,

Who do business on great waters;

They have seen the works of the Lord,

And His wonders in the deep.

THE BOOK OF PSALMS

AT THE SEASIDE

When I was down beside the sea,

A wooden spade they gave to me

To dig the sandy shore.

My holes were empty like a cup

In every hole the sea came up,

Till it could come no more.

ROBERT LOUIS STEVENSON

I will make you brooches

and toys for your delight

Of bird-song at morning

and star-shine at night.

I will make a palace

fit for you and me

Of green days in forests

and blue days at sea.

Robert Louis Stevenson

Variations old and new

D. Morgan © 1993

His rhapsody in green and blue.

A livelier emerald twinkles in the grass

A livelier emerald twinkles in the grass

A purer sapphire melts into the sea.

ALFRED, LORD TENNYSON

Blue Days at Sea

The crying gulls ～

The thundering surf ～

As I stood on the deck I could see

several other ships sailing out on the

evening tide, some quite close, cleaving

through the water abreast of us only

a few hundred yards away,

a graceful and thrilling sight.

JAMES HERRIOT
The Lord God Made Them All

All are ....

..... Music to my ears.

The song of the sea......

On the shore a child was standing,

Gazing o'er the sparkling sea,

And the sunset's rosy beauty

Filled her little heart with glee.

Far away a sail was moving

On the water, heaving bright,

And it crossed the orb so brilliant,

Ere it sank away from sight.

In an awe-struck, joyous whisper

Lisped the artless little thing;

"Oh! It is the door of heaven,

For I saw an angel's wing!"

GERTRUDE B. DUFFER

It was with a happy heart that the good

Odysseus spread his sail to catch the wind...

HOMER, *The Odyssey*

D. Morgan © 1993

Here with each new sunrise, life begins anew.

Its sweet retired bay, backed by dark cliffs,

where fragments of low rock among the sands

make it the happiest spot for watching the flow of the tide,

for sitting in unwearied contemplation...

must be visited, and visited again...

JANE AUSTEN, *Persuasion*

D. Morgan © 1996

THE BEACH

See! I have a little shovel,

I also have a pail,

And I have a little sailboat

That has a tiny sail.

I take them to the beach with me

But always do forget

To play with them, because you see

I'm busy getting wet.

ANONYMOUS

Linger by the sea, where worldly cares are few.

*D*own at the base of the cliffs were heaps

of surf—worn rocks or little sandy coves

inlaid with pebbles as with ocean jewels;

beyond lay the sea, shimmering and blue,

and over it soared the gulls, their pinions

flashing silvery in the sunlight.

"*I*sn't the sea wonderful?" said Anne....

"Don't you think it would be nice

to wake up at sunrise and swoop down

over the water and away out over that

lovely blue all day; and then at night

to fly back to one's nest?

Oh, I can just imagine doing it."

L.M. MONTGOMERY
Anne of Green Gables

Through the ⚓ *storm*

D. Morgan © 1987

The sea called ever to the dwellers on shore,
and even those who might not answer its call felt the thrill
and unrest and mystery and possibilities of it.

L.M. MONTGOMERY, *Anne's House of Dreams*

.... You do not walk alone.

Majestic Music

His orchestration of the sea...

To walk along the beach—

The sun against your face—

Feels every bit as sweet

As the warmth of an embrace.

D. MORGAN

D. Morgan © 1998

A mesmerizing symphony.

The woods call to us with a hundred

voices, but the sea has one only—

a mighty voice that drowns our souls

in its majestic music. The woods are human,

but the sea is of the company

of the archangels.

L.M. MONTGOMERY
Anne's House of Dreams

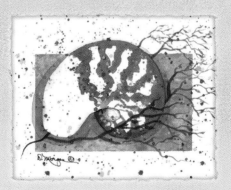

Reminders of the carefree days building castles — in — the sand.
D. Morgan

I have seen a curious child, who dwelt upon a tract

Of inland ground, applying to his ear

The convolutions of a smooth-lipped shell,

To which, in silence hushed, his very soul

Listened intensely; and his countenance soon

Brightened with joy, for from within were heard

Murmurings, whereby the monitor expressed

Mysterious union with its native sea.

WILLIAM WORDSWORTH
"The Excursion"

These tiny shells are treasures — held so close in hand.
D. Morgan

When I see the miracle

I know God

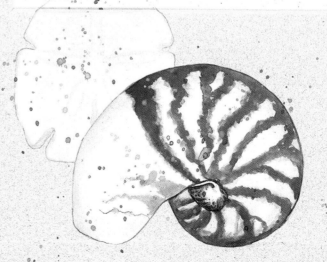

...Must

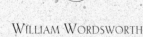

I wiped away the weeds and foam,

I fetched me sea-born treasures home.

RALPH WALDO EMERSON

Each day a new ~ beginning ~ filled ~ with ~ serenity

Of a shell —

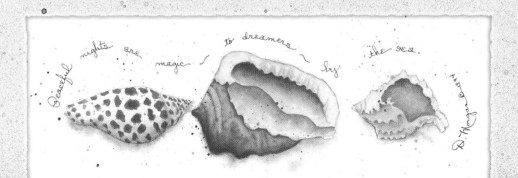

and nature...

Surely Touch Hands.

D. Morgan ©1990

A shell—how small an empty space,
a folding out of pink and white,
a letting in of spiral light.
How random? and how commonplace?
(A million shells along the beach
are just as fine and full of grace
as this one here within your reach.)

But lift it, hold it to your ear
and listen. Surely you can hear
the swish and sigh of all the grey
and gleaming waters, and the play
of wind with rain and sun, encased
in one small jewel box and placed,
by God and oceans, in your way.

LUCI SHAW

Peaceful nights are magic ~ to dreamers ~ by ~ the sea.

I walked far down the beach, soothed

by the rhythm of the waves...the wind

and mist from the spray on my hair.

ANNE MORROW LINDBERGH
Gift From the Sea

Soothed by the Rhythm

of the Waves

How sweet ~ The Salty... ...Air.

D. Morgan ©1990

My life is like a stroll upon the beach,

As near the ocean's edge as I can go.

HENRY DAVID THOREAU, *The Fisher's Boy*

The old man knew he was going far

out and he left the smell of the land behind

and rowed out into the clean

early morning smell of the ocean.

ERNEST HEMINGWAY
The Old Man and the Sea

When I am in my ship, I see

The other ships go sailing by

A sailor leans and calls to me

As his ship goes sailing by

Across the sea he leans to me,

Above the winds I hear him cry:

"Is this the way to Round-the-World?"

He calls as he goes by.

A.A. MILNE
When We Were Very Young

Each new wave

Rearranges

D. Morgan © 1990

.....So we may pretend
Our footsteps
Are
The
First.

The sea has many voices.

T.S. ELIOT

the patterns in the sand.....

The scene was more beautiful far to the eye

Than if the day in its pride had arrayed it.

And o'er them the lighthouse looked lovely as hope,—

That star of life's tremulous ocean.

PAUL MOON JAMES

Guiding friendly strangers,
The
Keeper
Of
The
Lighthouse

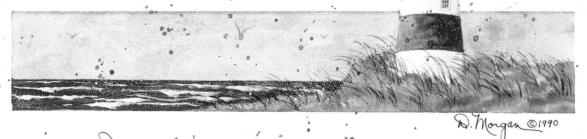

Is surely...

...Friends with God.

D. Morgan ©1990